The END TIMES

A HISTORICAL PERSPECTIVE

D. JAMES KENNEDY, PH.D.

The End Times
A Historical Perspective

By D. James Kennedy, Ph.D.

Edited by Karen VanTil Gushta, Ph.D.

Copyright © 2016 D. James Kennedy Ministries.

ISBN: 978-1-929626-72-4

Cover and Interior Design: Roark Creative, www.roarkcreative.com

Printed in the United States of America.

Published by:

D. James Kennedy Ministries
P.O. Box 11786
Fort Lauderdale, FL 33339
1-800-988-7884
DJKM.org
letters@djkm.org

TABLE OF CONTENTS

FOREWORD..5

CHAPTER ONE
THE SECOND COMING..7

CHAPTER TWO
THE TIME OF THE RAPTURE..17

CHAPTER THREE
THE TRIBULATION..33

CHAPTER FOUR
THE THIEF IN THE NIGHT..47

CHAPTER FIVE
THE LAST TRUMPET..65

CHAPTER SIX
THE MILLENNIUM...77

FOREWORD

Many years ago, I asked Dr. Kennedy for his views on the *eschaton*—that's the fancy Greek word for the last days, the end of human history, the consummation of all things. From this root we get the word eschatology—the study of last things. By way of answering my question, Dr. Kennedy pointed me to the Old Testament Scriptures—specifically the hundreds of prophecies concerning the coming of Messiah. These messianic prophecies were widely known in ancient Israel. They were studied, and memorized—and not just by scribes, priests, and scholars. All devout Jewish families made the memorization of Scripture a central part of family life and devotion.

Any serious study of these prophecies took great effort, because the Old Testament contains 333 prophecies concerning the coming of Christ. Here is a notable example written some 700 years before the birth of Jesus: *"For unto us a child is born, unto us a son is given, and the government shall be upon his shoulder. And his name shall be called Wonderful Counselor, Mighty God, Eternal Father, Prince of Peace"* (Isaiah 9:6).

Or consider this one: *"But He was wounded for our transgressions, he was bruised for our iniquities; the chastisement of our peace was upon him, and by his stripes we are healed. All of us like sheep have gone astray; each of us has turned to his own way, but the* LORD *has laid on him the iniquity of us all"* (Isaiah 53:5-6).

While these and other Messianic prophecies seem clear to us today, it was not so in Israel before Jesus' coming. References to the "Son" were often thought to refer to the nation of Israel as a whole. And even when they understood a passage to be about the person of Messiah, they misunderstood His purpose for coming.

We also have confusion in our day with respect to the

Second Coming of Jesus. Bible scholars of various theological persuasions look at the same prophecies, yet they often reach dramatically different conclusions about them.

And here was Dr. Kennedy's point: It was only by the light of Jesus' incarnation that these prophecies became clear. In the same way, only by the light of Jesus' Second Coming will we fully understand the prophecies about it.

This does not mean we cannot know anything about the Lord's return. In fact, there are three central truths about the return of Jesus Christ that no serious Bible student disputes. He will return: *visibly* (Revelation 1:7); *bodily* (Acts 1:11); and *gloriously* (1 Thessalonians 4:16-17. And there is a great deal more we can know as well.

While church history reveals a diversity of opinion on the Second Coming of Jesus, there has always been a majority view on what the Scriptures teach about His return. This majority view is the theological perspective Dr. Kennedy advances in the messages that follow. It represents the most widely-held view of the church throughout the nearly 2000-year history of Christendom—even though it is not the most widely-held view today.

Let me be clear on this point: the aim of these messages is NOT to persuade you to Dr. Kennedy's personal viewpoint. It is that you would consider the Scriptures and be persuaded by them alone. May you be blessed as you reflect and meditate on these things! And may you not forget the promise of the angels standing on the Mount of Olives: *"They said, "Men of Galilee, why stand looking toward Heaven? This same Jesus, who was taken up from you to Heaven, will come in like manner as you saw Him go into Heaven"* (Acts 1:11).

Frank Wright, Ph.D.
President and CEO,
D. James Kennedy Ministries

CHAPTER ONE

THE SECOND COMING

As were the days of Noah, so will be the coming of the Son of Man. For as in the days before the flood, they were eating and drinking, marrying and giving in marriage, until the day Noah entered the ark, and did not know until the flood came and took them all away, so will be the coming of the Son of Man.

MATTHEW 24:37-39

The study of last things is called "eschatology." In the Greek language, the word "eschaton" means "the end." Thus, eschatology is the study of "the end." We live in a time when there is a great interest in this subject. In our time, there is considerable attention drawn to and focused upon the end of the world and the Second Coming of Jesus Christ.

My focus here will be on the subject of when Christ is going to come again for His own. I'd like to have you follow with me in the Bible in these matters because there are a number of diverse theories concerning when Jesus Christ is going to come back. For example, there are those who say that Jesus will come back again for His own a thousand and seven years before the end of the world. That's one theory.

Then there is another theory that says He will come back a thousand and three-and-a-half years before the end of the world. And there is a third theory, which says He will come back a thousand years before the end of the world. That's seven, three-and-a-half, and a thousand even. Finally, there is another view that says He will come back at the end of the world—that the return of Jesus Christ will be the culmination of all things and will usher in the final lowering of the curtain upon the world as we know it, and the beginning of the eternal ages in paradise for some and in hell for others.

What Does the Bible Teach?

Now, having said that there are numerous theories like this, we might suppose that the Bible is rather vague about this subject, or unclear. I do not think that this is the case. I think that the Bible is, indeed, quite clear as to when Jesus Christ will come. In the following chapters, I will present distinct strands of evidence from the major passages that deal with the Second Coming of Christ for His own. We will consider what they say about when this will happen. It is quite clear to me that each one of these passages teaches exactly the same thing. And, that when wound together, these various strands provide one unbreakable strand of biblical evidence as to when this will take place. I do not want to set before you my theory or opinion. But the view I will present has been the view that has been the most widely and historically held in the Church down through 20 centuries. And it is also the view set forth in the Westminster Confession of Faith.

Nonetheless, the important question is whether this is what the Bible teaches. This must be the final determiner in all questions of religion. What do the Scriptures teach about this matter? However, I believe that if you will look with me at each of these strands of Scripture, you will be brought to an irresistible conclusion. A conclusion which may surprise some of you, a conclusion which goes against many popular theories of our day. And yet it is a conclusion that I think is inescapable from the biblical evidence. That conclusion is that the Bible clearly teaches that the Second Coming of Jesus Christ will be the consummation of all things. He will come at the end of the world, and the day that the Lord Jesus Christ comes back to this earth will be the Last Day. It will be the end of all things— the final climacteric of the ages.

The Classic Passage

We want to take a look at some of the passages that deal with the subject, beginning with 1 Thessalonians 4. In this chapter, we have the classic passage dealing with the coming of Christ for His own. This is sometimes called the Rapture. The word "rapture" is not found in the Bible. It is not a biblical term, so some prefer the more biblical term "the return of the Lord." Be that as it may, the word rapture is taken from a Latin word which means "to snatch away," or "to catch away."

In 1 Thessalonians 4:16-17, we read, *"For the Lord Himself will descend from heaven with a shout, with the voice of the archangel, and with the trumpet call of God. And the dead in Christ will rise first. Then we who are alive and remain shall be caught up together with them in the clouds to meet the Lord in the air. And so shall we be forever with the Lord."* The Lord tells us that He is going to come back and He is going to catch up those who truly believe in Him into the air to be with Him forever.

Now, when is this going to happen? Is it, indeed, at the end of the world, or is it some period before that? In the 24th chapter of Matthew, Jesus deals with this subject. In Matthew 24:7 we read, *"For as in the days before the flood, they were eating and drinking, and marrying and giving in marriage, until the day Noah entered the ark, and did not know until the flood came and took them all away, so will be the coming of the Son of Man."*

As in the Days of Noah

We are told here that the coming of the Son of Man will be as it was in the days of Noah. We're told also that in the day that the flood came upon the earth, *"they did not know"* until it came and took them away. Now we read in Genesis 7 that God commanded Noah and his sons and their wives to go into the ark. He tells him in Genesis 7:1, *"You and your entire household go into the ark, for you alone I have seen to be righteous before Me among this generation."* God also tells Noah, *"In seven days I will cause it to rain on the earth for forty days and forty nights."* And He commands him to take seven of every clean animal and two of every unclean animal.

Noah obeyed the command and during those seven days we have the gathering into the ark of every animal that walks and creeps upon the earth. When those seven days were completed, males and females of all flesh that was upon the earth had entered the ark. Then in Genesis 7:11-13 we read: *"In the six hundredth year of Noah's life, in the second month, the seventeenth day of the month, the same day, all the fountains of the great deep burst open and the floodgates of the heavens were opened. The rain fell upon the earth for forty days and forty nights. On the very same day Noah and the sons of Noah, Shem and Ham and Japheth, and Noah's wife, and the three wives of his sons with them, entered the ark."*

A Picture of the Coming of the Lord

Here we have a great picture of the coming of the Lord—so shall it be when the Son of Man comes. We have a picture of the judgment upon the earth, a preview of the final judgment: when fire shall fall upon the earth and destroy the world and when all of the wicked shall be destroyed. Noah and his family represent a picture of the Church, of the true believers, of those who are made righteous, by faith in God. And we see that they were taken out of this terrible destruction that came upon the world, this wrath of God that fell upon mankind.

When did this happen? Were Noah and his family taken

out a long time before the coming of the destruction? No. We are told that in the self-same day in which the fountains of the great deep burst open and the floodgates of the heavens were opened, in that same day when the rain came upon the earth, Noah and his wife, and his sons, and their wives entered into the ark and were saved. And so it shall be with the coming of the Son of Man. Jesus Christ shall come and take His own into the safety of His own presence in the day in which the wrath of God shall fall upon the earth.

Two Concepts Are Often Confused

It is important that we distinguish here between two concepts that are sometimes confused: the concept of 'tribulation' and the concept of 'wrath.' The Bible says that we shall have tribulation. *"In the world you will have tribulation. But be of good cheer. I have overcome the world"* (John 16:33). But the Bible also says that we are not appointed unto wrath. The Children of Israel, for example, were in Egypt when the tribulation came upon that nation, but they were not in Egypt when the wrath of God destroyed the entire army of Egypt altogether. And so here, we're not dealing with tribulation, but we are dealing with the wrath of God, which destroyed the people of the earth entirely—each and every one. (And by the way, historians estimate that there were hundreds of millions of people on the earth, based on computations of birth rates at that time, who were destroyed in the universal flood.)

This was a great outpouring of the wrath of God upon the world, and a reminder of the fact that though sin should become ever so popular, and people should join hand in hand against God, God is not impressed. You can't form a union against God. God has destroyed the world once in the past, and He will destroy it again in the future. But those who believe in Christ and trust in Him have this same promise that even as God brought Noah and his family into the ark in the same day when the rains of destruction and wrath fell upon the earth, so Jesus Christ, who is the true Ark of safety will come for His own and take them unto Himself in that day when the rains will fall upon this world for the last time. The rains of His fire and wrath—in the self-same day.

I believe you will find that as we consider each of the Scripture passages that deal with this subject, the very same truth is taught over and over and over and over again in a mounting crescendo. All of our questions will not be answered at once, but I would urge you to patiently continue in the study of what God has to say about this matter. So I trust that when we have completed this subject, you will see clearly what the Word of God says about this matter—that Jesus Christ will come again for His own, and that will be the consummation of the ages and the end of the world. And I hope that you will be ready.

A PRAYER...

Father, even now the storm clouds are gathering. Help us not to be as those who are blind and do not see, but be children of light—children who watch and wait, and children who can say, "Even so, Lord Jesus, come quickly." To the glory of Your most blessed Name, Amen.

CHAPTER TWO

THE TIME OF THE RAPTURE

For the Lord Himself will descend from heaven with a shout, with the voice of the archangel, and with the trumpet call of God. And the dead in Christ will rise first. Then we who are alive and remain shall be caught up together with them in the clouds to meet the Lord in the air. And so we shall be forever with the Lord.

1 THESSALONIANS 4:16-17

It's not often that I speak on this subject. But many people have asked numerous questions in recent months, and there is a great deal of interest in the subject of eschatology, the "last things." It is a subject that has attracted the attention of men for many centuries and we seem to have an insatiable curiosity about it and a desire to know the future. In the secular world, Spurgeon said that this curiosity was satisfied by those who read tea leaves, and go to palm readers and fortune tellers, and read the astrological charts. Some people have the same penchant in the theological sphere, but nevertheless, we do need to from time to time, look at the future—the glorious future that God has prepared for us.

Let Us Examine the Biblical Evidence

Today a gentleman called me and said that he had seen the title of my message in the newspaper and he wanted to find out which of the four views I held before he decided whether or not he was going to come. I wouldn't tell him—I figured I only had one in four chances of picking the one that he wanted to hear. I did tell him that I was going to present the biblical evidence for what I thought the Bible taught about this matter, and I hoped that he would have an open mind to come and hear that regardless of what view he held.

It would be very sad if we get to the place where we have become so close-minded about this topic that we are no longer able in Christian love to discuss such a matter. You know, there are some things about which all Christians agree. But there are other instances where this is not the case. There is a great saying, which I have adopted as my own: "In essentials, unity. In non-essentials, liberty. And in all things, charity, or love." And

I think that's a good rule to try to follow.

Now, it is, no doubt true that good, sincere, godly, intelligent Christians have disagreed about the matter we're considering, and I think that we need to recognize that fact. Also, you need to know that I am not infallible, and I am going to present to you the evidence as I see it. Now, I want you to ignore my opinion about the matter, and I want you to examine the weight of biblical evidence.

Four Views of the Time of Jesus' Return

Keep in mind when we talk about the time of the "Rapture," we're obviously not talking about a calendar date. I'm not talking about October 2, 1986, or something like that. We're actually talking about time as it relates to the agenda of God, so to speak, concerning the events that will take place in the Last Days, as we're told in the Bible.

Basically, there are four views that have been set forth concerning the time when Jesus Christ is going to come— which has been called (and I use that term here), the time of the "Rapture." The word comes from a Latin word that means "to snatch away," or "take away," and I prefer the more biblical term of "the return of Christ," or "the coming of the Lord," but, nevertheless, for understanding on the part of many, I use the term "Rapture."

Let's say that this is the end of the world—the *consummation* of all things, the Last Days when God drops the curtain upon this world. There are those who have held that Christ would come again for His own, which is specifically what is meant by the term "Rapture," to take out His own unto Himself. There are those who have said that this would happen a thousand and seven years before the consummation. There are those who have said, secondly, that it would happen a thousand and three and a half years before the consummation. Thirdly, there are those that have said that it would happen a thousand years before the consummation. And there are those who have said that it would happen at the Last Day, at the consummation, at the conclusion of all things.

We Must Search the Scriptures

As I pointed out previously in speaking of "The Second Coming," the testimony of the Scripture points to the fact that the Rapture will take place on the Last Day. I hope that we will not be blinded by previously conceived systems so we are not willing to look at the actual testimony of the Scripture. I believe that the Bible is not obscure at this particular point at all. It very clearly states when this is going to take place.

I am going to take the major passages in the Bible that deal with this subject and set forth one after another to show the strands of evidence concerning this matter, and I trust that you will see that they weave themselves into a very strong chord. Obviously, not all of the evidence can be presented here, and I certainly don't feel that the case will have been fully made until all of the evidence is in. Furthermore, I should point out the fact that it is inevitable that there must be some interpretation of Scripture. Everyone must interpret the Scripture when they read it and I must interpret it when I preach it. And I realize that everything I say isn't the way it is, *ipse dixit*; i.e., "it is said," and that's the end of it. There is, of course, some interpretation involved. But I hope that you'll be able to follow and evaluate for yourself. One thing I ask and that is: "search the Scriptures," and see whether or not these things be so.

God Saves a Remnant

We started with a passage that dealt with Noah and the flood. Jesus said, "*As were the days of Noah, so will be the coming of the Son of Man*" (Matthew 24:37). The Bible says that seven days before the flood came, God commanded Noah to gather together the unclean beasts, two of each kind, and seven of the clean and to bring them into the ark. Genesis tells us specifically what happened. Here's a picture of God saving this little remnant, which is symbolic of the Church being taken out of the midst of an ungodly world upon which He is going to rain destruction and death.

When did this happen? When were they taken out of this destruction? Genesis tells us that in the 600th year of Noah's life, in the second month, the 17th day of the month, the same day were all of the fountains of the great deep broken up and the windows of heaven were opened, and the rain was upon the earth 40 days and 40 nights. In the self-same day, entered Noah and Shem, Ham, and Japheth, the sons of Noah, and Noah's wife and the three wives of his sons into the ark. Luke 17 tells us that people were eating and drinking and so on, until "the day" in which Noah entered into the ark and the water came and carried them all away. So the taking of the believers into the ark took place on the self-same day in which God brought destruction upon the world and carried them all away. That was our first piece of evidence.

The Time of the Rapture

Now I want to move to the heart of the matter, to that passage that is most frequently dealt with when people speak of the Rapture; one found in 1 Thessalonians 4:16-17, where it says, *"For the Lord Himself will descend from Heaven with a shout, with the voice of the archangel, and with the trumpet call of God, And the dead in Christ will rise first. Then we who are alive and remain shall be caught up together with them in the clouds to meet the Lord in the air. And so we shall be forever with the Lord."*

Now, let's ask: in this immediate passage, do we have any clue as to when the time of this event is to be? I think we have a very definite and conclusive indication of when this is to be, right in the very heart of this passage itself. We do not have to look somewhere else, but right here in the passage it tells us when this is going to be. And that clue is found in the fact that when the Lord Himself descends from Heaven, we find that the dead in Christ shall rise first, then we which are alive and remain shall be caught up. So when Christ comes to catch up His own, we see that is when the dead in Christ are resurrected. Does anybody have any question in their mind, as you read this passage that Christ's coming and descending from Heaven with a shout and catching up believers in the air is going to take place at the same time as the resurrection of believers? The scripture says: For the Lord Himself will descend from heaven with a shout, with the voice of the archangel, and with the trumpet call of God. *And the dead in Christ will rise first. Then we who are alive and remain shall be caught up together with them in the clouds."* I think that is without controversy.

So now, when is that going to be? Is that going to be a thousand and seven years before the end? Is that going to be a thousand and three and a half years? A thousand? Or is that going to be at *the end*—the end of the world? Could it be at the very last day of the world? What does the Scripture say?

The Last Day

God tells us very clearly when this event will take place. In John chapter 6:39, Jesus said, *"This is the will of the Father who sent Me, that of all which He has given Me, I should lose nothing, but should raise it up again at the last day."* Now here is a very specific term—"the Last Day"—*he eschate hemera*. On that day He says He should raise up all of those whom the Father has given Him. On "the Last Day." Not some period a long time before that, but at "the Last Day." This phrase is used seven times in the New Testament. One of those times it refers to the last day of the feast, the Feast of the Tabernacles, but the other six times refers to the Last Day generally—the Last Day of the world. And what happens on "the Last Day"?

In verse 40 of John 6, we read, *"This is the will of Him who sent Me, that everyone who sees the Son and believes in Him may have eternal life, and I will raise Him up at the last day."* The *eschate hemera*—the Last Day. In verse 44 of the same chapter, *"No one can come to Me unless the Father who has sent Me draws him. And I will raise him up at the last day."* Verse 54, *"Whoever eats My flesh and drinks My blood has eternal life. And I will raise him up on the last day."* Now here are four verses in one chapter, each one of which deals with the resurrection of believers—those who have eternal life; those who see the Son and believe upon Him; those whom the Father has given Him; and those that should not be lost. These believers are the dead in Christ who will be raised up at the Last Day.

The Rapture Is on the Last Day

Is it not now the inescapable conclusion that the dead are raised up at the Last Day and Jesus Christ catches up His own on the Last Day? As 1 Thessalonians says, *"And the dead in Christ will rise first. Then we who are alive and remain shall be caught up together with them in the clouds to meet the Lord in the air."* If these things happen at the same time, can we escape the conclusion that it's saying that it is at the Last Day when the Lord comes that He will take us up to be with Him in the air? So the time of the Rapture is apparently clearly indicated to be *on the Last Day.*

As I noted previously there are seven places where the term, "the Last Day," is used in the New Testament, one of which refers to the Feast of Tabernacles. There are six then, that deal with the Last Day. We have looked at four. There is another one in the gospel of John, John 11:24, which is the familiar passage dealing with the resurrection of Lazarus. Chapter 11, verses 23 and 24 tell of the conversation between Jesus and Martha concerning her brother. *"Jesus said to her, 'Your brother shall rise again.'"* Martha said to Him, *"I know that he shall rise again in the resurrection on the Last Day."* Here again, we see that the resurrection will take place at the Last Day.

Judgment Is on the Last Day

There is one other passage in John that deals with this same phrase, this specific phrase that God uses very precisely—the

Last Day—as a clearly delineated time. John 12:48, "*He who rejects Me, and does not receive My words, has that which judges him. The word that I have spoken, the same will judge him on the last day.*" Here is the same phrase, "the last day," *he eschate hemera.* We notice here that something else is going to take place on the last day; there will be a judgment of those who have rejected Christ—the unbelievers will be judged on the Last Day. If the unbelievers are to be judged on the Last Day, then obviously they must have been resurrected first, for we know that the Bible clearly teaches that the judgment does not take place until after people have been resurrected. Therefore, we can know that on the Last Day, we have the resurrection of the unsaved dead, as well. So we have the resurrection both of believers and of unbelievers on the Last Day, and the judgment of unbelievers is here specifically said to take place on the Last Day. Therefore, we see a resurrection both of the saved and the lost that is to take place on the Last Day.

This is more specifically stated in both aspects in John, chapter 5. In John 5:25 and 28 and 29, both the saved and the lost are dealt with: "*Truly, truly I say to you, the hour is coming, and is now here, when all the dead will hear the voice of the Son of God, and those who hear will live. . . . Do not marvel at this. For the hour is coming in which all who are in the graves will hear His voice and come out—those who have done good to the resurrection of life, and those who have done evil to the resurrection of judgment.*"

Everyone Will Hear His Voice

Notice what these verses teach. There is an hour coming, a small period of time, in which all that are in the graves shall hear His voice. Previously, we noticed in Thessalonians that the

Lord will descend from Heaven with a shout, and when Christ comes with a shout, everyone is going to hear His voice, both the saved and the lost, and the graves will be opened and both will come forth. The bodies of the saved will come forth and will be caught up into the air to meet their own souls, which have already gone to be with the Lord and which Christ will bring with Him, as it says there in 1 Thessalonians. The unsaved will be raised upon the earth to endure destruction that is coming upon the earth. So we see that all of those in the graves will hear His voice and come forth—some to the resurrection of life and some to the resurrection of damnation.

We should also note here that some people teach that 1 Thessalonians 4 is teaching a "silent" Rapture, or a "secret" Rapture, and in the literature both of those terms are used to describe the Rapture. But my friends, as one has well commented, 1 Thessalonians 4 is one of the noisiest passages in all of Scripture! *"The Lord Himself will descend from Heaven with a shout, with the voice of the archangel, and with the trumpet call of God."* That's going to be a very, very noisy day. It's going to be a startling day for many. So apparently, there is nothing secret about it when Christ comes on the Last Day.

More than One Judgment?

We noticed in John that it says that those who have rejected Christ will be judged. So what does the Bible teach about this matter of judgment? There are those that say that there are a number of different judgments that take place at different times, and at one time in my life I believed that to be true myself. Then I took it upon myself to go through the Scripture and examine carefully every single verse in the

Bible that deals with the judgment, and I found that on more than a score of times, the Bible clearly teaches that there is a judgment coming—a single judgment. The Bible never speaks of judgments, but simply of the judgment or a day of judgment when God will judge the world, and present at that day (as clearly seen in numerous passages) will be both the saved and the lost *in the same judgment.*

As further evidence for that fact, you might turn to Romans chapter 2. Here we see in verses 5 and 6: *"But because of your hardness and impenitent heart, you are storing up treasures of wrath against yourself on the day of wrath when the righteous judgment of God will be revealed, and He will render to every man according to his deeds."* Now, there are people who have a certain theory that they want to uphold, so whenever they see a passage like this they say, "Well, that has to be the saved, or it has to be the lost, but it can't be both, because they both never appear at the same judgment." And, as I say, that was my opinion for a number of years.

The Light of Scripture

However, I do not believe that this view stands up to the light of Scripture. Who is it that is here? Is it the saved or the lost? Well, read on. *"To those who by patiently doing good seek for glory and honor and immortality will be eternal life. But unto those who are contentious and do not obey the truth, but obey unrighteousness, indignation and wrath, will be tribulation and anguish, upon every soul of man who does evil, to the Jew first, and then to the Gentile."* [Then Paul states again], *"But glory, honor, and peace to every man who does good work—to the Jew first, and then to the Gentile, for there is no partiality with God"* (Romans 2:7-11).

Or we find, for example, in Acts 17:30-31 another statement concerning this. Paul says, "*. . . but now He commands all men everywhere to repent. For He has appointed a day on which He will judge the world in righteousness by a Man whom He has appointed . . .*" God has appointed a day in which He will judge the world. Or, again, consider Revelation 11:18, "*The nations were angry and Your wrath has come, and the time for the dead to be judged, and to reward Your servants the prophets and the saints and those who fear Your name, small and great, and to destroy those who destroy the earth.*" So here again, at the time of the judgment both the saved and the lost are present.

Jesus Taught the Coming Judgment

Jesus taught this dozens of times. For example, in Matthew 11:22 Christ reprimanded the cities where most of His mighty works were done, saying, "*. . . it shall be more tolerable for Tyre and Sidon on the Day of Judgment than for you.*" And He said to Capernaum, "*But I say to you that it shall be more tolerable for the land of Sodom on the Day of Judgment, than for you*" (Matthew 11:24).

In Matthew 12:36-37, we see that Jesus said, "*But I say to you that for every idle word that men speak, they will give an account on the Day of Judgment. For by your words you will be justified, and by your words you will be condemned.*" Here some are justified and some are condemned on the day of judgment. And verse 41 says, "*The men of Nineveh will stand up at the judgment with this generation and will condemn it, because they repented at the teaching of Jonah. And now One greater than Jonah is here.*" The men of Nineveh who repented will rise up in the judgment and will condemn these wicked cities of Capernaum and so on, because they repented and these did not. However, they shall be *in the same judgment* and rise up and condemn the others at *that same judgment.*

Let's look at the parable of the talents recorded in Matthew 25. In that parable, at the judgment, the man with one talent and the man with two and the man with five are present. Of the one who has five talents and gained five more, the master said, *"Enter the joy of your master."* But to the one who had one talent and buried it, the master said, *"Take the talent from him, and give it to him who has ten talents . . . and throw the unprofitable servant into outer darkness,"* and he was cast out into outer darkness where there will be weeping and gnashing of teeth. Some enter into the blessedness of the Lord, and some go into outer darkness with weeping and gnashing of teeth.

Conclusion

There are scores of passages in the Bible that clearly teach that the saved and the lost will be present at the same judgment and will be judged together. What, then, may we conclude from this concerning the time of Christ's return? We can conclude this; that Jesus Christ will return at the Last Day—that day on which destruction will come upon the world. We can also notice that on that day, as the Bible says, the following things are to take place:

1. The dead in Christ will be raised; i.e., the resurrection of believers.

2. Living believers will be caught up, or "raptured," taken up to be with the Lord on that day.

3. Unbelievers will also be resurrected from the dead on that same day. The wicked, the living wicked, will be destroyed, as we noticed in the case of Noah that when the believers are taken out, then destruction, sudden destruction comes upon the world.

4. And lastly, all will be judged in that day; both the saved and the lost shall give an account of themselves before God in that Last Day.

All of these things make up one strand of the Scripture passages that deal with the time of the coming of Christ for His own. In my understanding of the Scripture, all teach the same thing—that the coming of Jesus Christ will be the culminating event upon this earth and will bring down the curtain on the drama of the ages. This will stop the wheel of time and usher in the endless ages of eternity. It will bring destruction upon the wicked and will bring about the final judgment on mankind.

A Prayer...

Heavenly Father, knowing that there is a day coming when all will be judged and must give an account before Jesus Christ, to whom all power and judgement is given, may we have greater zeal to reach those who are now in danger of eternal torments and punishment with the Gospel of Jesus Christ, so that they may join the righteous and receive fullness of joy as we enter Your presence. And may we always be watchful, for we know not the hour when the Lord will come, and may we be ever prepared to say, Come Lord Jesus, come quickly. Amen.

CHAPTER THREE

THE TRIBULATION

I have told you these things so that in Me you may have peace. In the world you will have tribulation. But be of good cheer. I have overcome the world.

JOHN 16:33

In looking at the coming of Jesus Christ, and more particularly that which is sometimes called the Rapture, we want to see how it relates to the other items on the agenda of God for the end times. We will now consider the coming of Christ and how it relates to a time of tribulation. The Bible indicates that in this world we have tribulation. It also indicates that tribulation will accelerate and will reach a climax at the end of the age, and so the question arises: How will that relate to the coming of Christ?

Now, you should understand historically what has been thought about this. Because, you know, a lot of times people have very little understanding of what has been the historical faith of the Church. They hear what is being said on radio and television, they read books that are being written today, and they have a rather horizontal view. They don't usually have an in-depth looking back through the centuries, a historical overview of what the Church has been and what it has believed. Consequently, sometimes people will accept novelties and suppose that they have been indeed the historic view of the Church. You should understand that down through the history of the Church, the Church has had a position concerning the relation between the Tribulation and the coming of Jesus Christ. And that position is quite different from the one which is very popular today.

The Church's Historic Position

The position of the Church historically has been that the Church would go through the Tribulation, and when that was completed, then Jesus Christ would come. Today, it is frequently taught in many circles that this is not the case and that Christ will come before the Tribulation and take the Church out of the world; and then there will be a period of tribulation; and then Christ will come again and bring an end to this age. That is a view that began in the spring of 1829. It began in a humble home in Scotland with a 16-year-old Scottish girl who had a vision. There was a revival going on in that town, a prayer meeting going on in that home, and John Nelson Darby and William Irving came and visited that home that year. Both of these men, the following year, in 1830, began to preach this new doctrine. And their preaching has been very persuasive, and it has become highly accepted in many areas of the Church today.

But you should understand that before 1829, this was not the view of the Church. Not Martin Luther, or John Calvin, or John Knox, or John Wesley, or any of the Reformers, or the Church Fathers believed this. Nor did the creeds of the Church state it. Historically, it was believed by the Church that there would be one Second Coming of Jesus Christ, and that it would occur after the "Tribulation."

"Tribulation" vs. "Wrath"

Now, we should understand what is meant by "tribulation," and should not confuse these two terms, which are sometimes confused by people. One is the matter of "tribulation," and the other is the matter of "wrath." Now, the Bible says that we have not been appointed unto wrath. The wrath is the destruction of God, which shall come upon the world and destroy the wicked and cast them everlastingly into perdition. Tribulation, however, is something quite different.

Let's look at John 16:33, which deals with tribulation. Here Jesus says something about the matter of tribulation. The word for wrath in Greek is *"orgé"*—the hot outpouring of the hatred of God for sin. The word for tribulation is *"thlipsis,"* which means distress or affliction. Jesus says in John 16:33, *"I have told you these things so that in Me you may have peace. In the world you will have tribulation. But be of good cheer. I have overcome the world."* Jesus said, *"In the world you will have tribulation."* Now, there are a number of texts in the Bible that deal with the subject of tribulation. There are also a number of texts in the Bible that deal with the coming of Jesus Christ for His own. We dealt with one of those in the previous chapter, and we should look at that again.

Playing Musical Chairs with Texts

In 1 Thessalonians 4:16, we have the classic text concerning what is called the Rapture. You see, the term Rapture originated after this young girl had her vision and Darby began to preach the two Second Comings of Jesus Christ. In order to distinguish between the two Second Comings, they didn't want to call it the Second Coming and the Third Coming, so they called it the Rapture and the Revelation. The classic text that they use for this is 1 Thessalonians 4:16-17 where we read, *"For the Lord Himself will descend from heaven with a shout, with the voice of the archangel, and with the trumpet call of God. And the dead in Christ will rise first. Then we who are alive and remain shall be caught up together with them in the clouds to meet the Lord in the air. And so we shall be forever with the Lord."*

Now, that's the classic passage. So, as I say, there are passages that deal with Tribulation, and there are passages that deal with the coming of Christ. But what has happened is that people have played musical chairs with these texts, because, you see, normally they're not found in the same book or in the same passage, the same chapter or paragraph in the Bible. So they will take passages that deal with the Tribulation, and they will say, "Well, let's put the coming of Christ—we'll take this from over in this book and we'll put it over here." And someone else says, "No, I think it goes over here." And another person says, "Well, I think it comes right here in the middle." And so you have developed three different views. Those that say it will come before the Tribulation, those that say it will come after the Tribulation, and those who are mid-Tribulationists, who hold that it will come in the middle.

Now you understand better what I meant when I said there are some who say Christ will come a thousand and seven years before the end of the age, a thousand and three, or a thousand years. And some will say He'll come at the end of the age.

The Tribulation and the Rapture

If there is a passage in the Bible that deals both with the Tribulation and with the Rapture, and which relates them together chronologically, then the musical chairs game is over, and we must say "Thus saith the Lord," and take what God has to say as the final word on that. There is such a passage, and it is found in Matthew 24. We read in the 21st verse, *"For then will be great tribulation, such as has not happened since the beginning of the world until now, no, nor ever shall be."* So we read there will be a time of great tribulation. In verse 30 of this chapter, we have a passage dealing with Christ coming for His own— what is called the Rapture. It says, *"Then the sign of the Son of Man will appear in heaven, and then all the tribes of the earth will mourn, and they will see the Son of Man coming on the clouds of heaven with power and great glory."*

Notice the comparison between 1 Thessalonians 4:16, which we just read concerning the Rapture, and this passage. In 1 Thessalonians it says, *"the Lord Himself will descend from heaven with a shout . . ."* Here in Matthew 24, we see that the Son of Man will be coming on clouds with power and great glory. We read in 1 Thessalonians that there would be the voice of the archangel. In Matthew 24:31, we read that He will send His angels. In Thessalonians we read that there would be the trumpet of God. Here in Matthew 24:31, we see that there will be "a great sound of a trumpet." And in Thessalonians we read that the dead in Christ and then the living in Christ should be gathered up to meet the Lord in the air. In Matthew we read that *"they shall gather His elect from the four winds, from one end of the heavens to the other."* This will be the gathering together of God's own unto Himself.

So the same four events take place. There is the Lord Himself descending from Heaven. There are the angels of God and the voice of the angel. There is, thirdly, the sound of the trumpet. And finally, there is the gathering together of His elect. This is what is known as the Rapture—Christ coming for His own.

The Time of the Tribulation and the Rapture

Now, the question is: Where does this appear chronologically with the Tribulation? Well, go back one verse to verse 29 of Matthew 24. There we read: "**Immediately after** the tribulation of those days, 'the sun will be darkened, the moon will not give its light; the stars will fall from heaven, and the powers of the heavens* *will be shaken.' **Then** the sign of the Son of Man in Heaven, and then all the tribes of the earth will mourn, and they shall see the Son of Man coming on the clouds of heaven with power and great glory . . . and they shall gather His elect."* Now, to my mind, my friends, though at one time I held a different view, this has ended all of my conjectures and all of my fantasies about the matter. This settled it. Whether I like it or I don't, if I believe the Word of God is the final authority in all religious questions, the matter is settled as far as I am concerned. It is *"immediately after the tribulation of those days"* that the Son of Man will come and gather together His elect unto Himself. And I really have difficulty seeing how anyone can get around that.

I remember that years ago, someone came over to my house, and they had just picked up the book, *The Late Great Planet Earth.* They were very excited about it, and they came over as if I had never heard of these things, and they wanted to enlighten me about it. So I said, "That's marvelous. I preached that twenty-some years ago. . . . That was before I made a thorough study of the Scriptures in the matter." "But," I said, "You know"—though I had not read the book then—"I would be willing to wager, if I were a betting man, that though there's only one passage in the Bible that deals conclusively with this matter, I will bet you that he doesn't even discuss it." And sure enough, we opened the book—silence, nothing, blank, not a word. Now my friends, I know he knows it's there. But why doesn't he deal with it? Thus saith the Lord: *"Immediately after the tribulation of those days."*

Are There Two Comings of Christ?

Another thing we are told in this view where we supposedly have two comings of Christ, is that in one of those comings

Jesus will come *for* His saints, and then He will come back seven years later *with* His saints. So we're told that in the Rapture, Christ comes for His saints, and then at the Revelation He comes all the way to the world with His saints. The passages that are used for this are again in 1 Thessalonians. Look at 1 Thessalonians 3:13: *"To this end may He establish your hearts to be blameless in holiness before our God and Father at the coming of our Lord Jesus Christ with all His saints."* So there is a passage that deals with Christ coming *with* all of His Saints. In 1 Thessalonians 4:16-17 it says that the Lord Himself shall descend and then we which are alive shall be caught up. In this passage it says Christ comes *for* His Saints.

So are there indeed two comings? Is there one coming where Christ comes *for* His Saints and is there another coming where He comes *with* His Saints? Well, I should point out to you first of all, that if there were, the Bible has the two reversed here and has the wrong one first, which presents a chronological problem right off the bat. But the real problem is a failure to note anything at all about what the Apostle is really speaking of, because in the passage in 1Thessalonians 4, which is the classic passage of the Rapture itself, in that passage there is the coming *with* the Saints *and* there is the coming *for* the Saints in the very same coming, a fact that seems to have been ignored or missed.

Christ Comes With Souls and For Bodies of Believers

Starting in verse 13 of 1 Thessalonians 4 we read, *"But I would not have you ignorant, brothers, concerning those who are asleep, that you may not grieve as others who have no hope. For if we believe that Jesus died and arose again, so God will bring with Him those who sleep in Jesus. For this we say to you by the word of the Lord, that we who are alive and remain until the coming of the Lord will not precede those who are asleep. For the Lord Himself will descend from heaven . . ."* (1 Thessalonians 4:13-16). Now what is He saying? He's simply saying this, that there are those that have died and their souls have gone to Heaven. When Jesus comes back again, He will come with the souls of all of those who have died, and He will come back to this world, and the graves will be opened and those souls will be joined unto the bodies of believers and then God will take them, body and soul, in their entirety to meet them in the air.

This is what the Bible is teaching, not that there are two separate comings, but in this one coming—in what is called the Rapture—we see that Christ comes both *with* the souls of the believers and *for* the bodies of the dead believers, and, of course, the entireties of those who still remain upon the earth.

When Will This Take Place?

Another thing that we might note if we go back to Matthew 24 again is the time when this happens. As Matthew 24 says, starting in verse 29, *"Immediately after the tribulation of those days, 'the sun will be darkened, and the moon will not give its light; the stars will fall from heaven, and the powers of the heavens will be shaken.' Then the sign of the Son of Man will appear in heaven . . . and they shall gather His elect . . ."* So when is it that Christ is going to come to gather together His own? When is it that the sun will be darkened and the moon will not give her light, and the stars will fall from heaven, and the powers of Heaven will be shaken? Well, you might turn to Revelation 6 to find out when that is going to be and what is going to happen.

In Revelation 6:12-17 we read about the opening of the 6th seal: *"I watched as He opened the sixth seal. And suddenly there was a great earthquake. The sun became black, like sackcloth made from goat hair, and the moon became like blood. And the stars of heaven fell to the earth, as a fig tree drops its unripe figs when it is shaken by a strong wind. Then the heavens receded like a scroll when it is rolled up, and every mountain and island was removed from its place. Then the kings of the earth and the great men and the rich men and the commanding officers and the strong and everyone, slave and free, hid themselves in the caves and in the rocks of the mountains. They said to the mountains and rocks, 'Fall on us, and hide us from the face of Him who sits on the throne, and from the wrath of the Lamb, for the great day of His wrath has come. Who is able to withstand it?'"*

By the way, you'll notice first of all, we see a very clear distinction in this passage; then, immediately after the Tribulation comes the wrath of God. This is obviously a clear picture of the final judgment day when God sits in final judgment. They asked to be hidden from the face of Him who sits on the throne and from the wrath of the Lamb. This is the Judgment Day.

What Happens on the Last Day?

Previously, in John 12:48 we saw that those who have rejected Him will be judged on the Last Day, *he eschate hemera*. And it was on the Last Day that Christ would raise all of the believers; those that the Father had given to Him would be raised up on the Last Day. We saw that on the Last Day was the day of the resurrection of the dead. We also saw in 1 Thessalonians 4:16 that one of the concomitant events happening with the coming of Jesus Christ is that the dead in Christ would be raised. There would be the resurrection of believers. When does that happen? It happens on the Last Day.

So what happens on the Last Day? Jesus Christ comes on the Last Day. The believers are raised on the Last Day. Unbelievers are raised on the Last Day. The unbelievers and all men are judged upon the Last Day. The stars of heavens fall from the sky, the sky is rolled up as a scroll, the sun ceases to give its light and the moon turns to blood on the Last Day. So we see that the coming of Jesus Christ for His own is on the Last Day of the earth.

I should say in conclusion, it is the same type of situation that you saw in Egypt during all of the time of the plagues; the Israelites were in the land in this time of affliction and tribulation. But when God finally poured out His wrath upon the Egyptian army and destroyed them entirely and completely, the children of Israel were out of the land. So we find the same is true for us. God knows how to take care of His own. God is able to keep His own.

In the World You Will Have Tribulation

Finally, I would say that I believe that there is a very, very unchristian, or false Christian attitude which is displayed, for example, in a man who said to me that the idea that Christians would be taken out of the world before the Tribulation was to him the most important doctrine in Christianity. I said to him,

"It is a novelty in the first place, and secondly, it is an unchristian attitude to display such a thing as that." My friends, Jesus said, *"In the world you will have tribulation. But be of good cheer. I have overcome the world,"* and down through the centuries and until this day, people have suffered great tribulation for Christ's sake.

"Shall we be carried to the skies on flowery beds of ease while others fought to win the prize and sailed through bloody seas?" Shall we go to that martyr that I think of in the times of the Roman persecution who simply came to claim the body of a brother of his who had been killed. And they said to him, "You are a Christian also." He said, "Yes." They said, "Deny Him." He said, "I cannot." So they took him out and they peeled every inch of skin off his body. Then they brought him back and they said, "Deny Christ." He said, "I cannot." They took him out, and they tied him to a spit and over a small fire of coals, hour after hour, they slowly broiled him, and he never made an outcry. I want to tell you, which one of you is going to go to that fellow there on that spit after four or five hours of broiling, having been peeled, and say to him, "Friend, be of good cheer, the Church is not going through the Tribulation?"

A Prayer...

Father, may we be good soldiers of Jesus Christ, willing to endure hardness, willing to stand for Him, whatever comes. We thank You, Lord, that we are your own and that you know how to take care of Your own, and even now, standing in the darkness, you are watching over your own, and you have promised that nothing shall separate us from Your love. So we rejoice, oh Christ, that it is our privilege even to suffer for You. Help us, we pray, to be faithful followers of the Lamb, whithersoever He leads. We pray this to the glory and honor of the name of Jesus Christ, to Him to Whom be praise forever more. Amen.

CHAPTER FOUR
THE THIEF IN THE NIGHT

Watch therefore, for you do not know what hour your Lord will come. But know this, that if the owner of the house had known what hour the thief would come, he would have watched and not have let his house be broken into. Therefore you also must be ready, for in an hour when you least expect, the Son of Man is coming.

MATTHEW 24:42-44

In this series dealing with eschatology, I have principally focused on when Jesus Christ is coming back again. We have said that there have basically been four different opinions as to when Christ will return again. Some have said that if this is the end, Christ would come back a thousand and seven years before the end. Others say it will be a thousand and three years; others a thousand, and still others have said that He would come back at the very end, or on the Last Day.

Now, obviously, *when* Christ comes back is going to influence what happens both before Christ comes and after He comes. Quite evidently, if He comes back on the Last Day, then nothing is going to happen after He comes except the ushering in of the eternal states of Heaven and Hell. If, however, He first comes back a thousand years before Christ returns, then that would be the position of those who would say that the Tribulation would come before Christ comes back, and then a thousand-year millennium would take place after that. If there are those that say He comes back after a thousand and seven years, they say that Christ will come back, and then there will be a period of tribulation for seven years, and then there will be a thousand-year period of a millennium.

As you know, I believe from my searching of the Scriptures— though I did not always hold this opinion—I hold to the position that has been most generally held through the centuries by the Church, which is, namely, that Jesus Christ will come back at the end of the Last Day. And therefore there will be nothing after His coming except the ushering in of the final states of Heaven and Hell. There will be the Resurrection and Judgment and Heaven and Hell.

Major Lines of Evidence

We have been setting forth the major lines of evidence that deal with the coming of Christ. We began with Noah—and to briefly recapitulate—let me remind you of the three strands of evidence that we've already looked at so that your mind will be stirred up by way of remembrance. We notice that we're told that the coming of Christ would be as it was in the days of Noah, and so this is one evidence that points to the coming of Christ. Noah and his wife and children and their wives were a picture of the remnant Church, which was taken out of the world before the wrath of God descended.

The question is: when did that happen? Genesis tells us that in the 600th year of Noah's life, in the second month on the 17th day that the fountains of the great deep were broken up and the windows of heaven were opened and the waters came upon the earth. Then we're told that in the selfsame day entered Noah and his wife and his sons and their wives into the ark. So when were they taken out of the world? In the very last day before the world was entirely destroyed. Luke 17:27 also reminds us that the people were eating and drinking and giving in marriage and so on, until the day that Noah entered into the ark and the rain came upon the earth. So that is when that happened.

Some Taken, Others Left Behind

Matthew 24 is often used to support the idea that some are going to be taken out, and then all these other things are going to happen. We read in verses 40 and 41, *"Two will be in the field; one will be taken, and the other left. Two women will be grinding at the mill; one will be taken, and the other left."* Well, as some have said, "a text without a context is a pretext." Look at the context and you will notice that these verses come right after the passage that speaks of the days of Noah. *"As were the days of Noah, so will be the coming of the Son of Man"* (Matthew 24:37). This whole passage is describing the way it was in the days of Noah.

Noah was taken out, and his wife was taken out, and his sons were taken out, and other people were left. That, of course, is absolutely true. When Christ comes back He will take His own to be with Himself. But the others are going to be left for . . . what? A picnic? What were the people in the days of Noah that were not taken out left for? Sudden destruction, which came upon them. In the selfsame day that fountains of the great deep were opened and the windows of Heaven, and they were all swept away. This is the context of those verses. So we see that the first passage that deals with the coming of the Son of Man points out that the believers will be taken out in the very day in which destruction comes upon the world.

Time Clues for the Rapture

The second passage that we turned to was the classic passage dealing with the so-called Rapture. You'll recall that those who decided that there would be two Second Comings of Christ called the first one the Rapture and the second one the Revelation, and that is found in 1 Thessalonians 4:14-17. And we asked if there was any chronological note, any time clue in that passage, and you will recall that there very definitely is. In 1 Thessalonians 4 we see that there is something that happens very clearly when this great event occurs and Christ Himself

51

descends from Heaven. As we read, *"For the Lord Himself will descend from heaven with a shout, with the voice of the archangel, and with the trumpet call of God. And the dead in Christ will rise first* [The dead in Christ will rise first!] *Then we who are alive and remain shall be caught up together with them in the clouds to meet the Lord in the air."* What is going to happen first? The dead in Christ are going to rise from the dead. So we see that the time clue in this very passage is very explicit—it is the resurrection of the believing dead.

When does that take place? The Gospel of John is very specific, and you will remember that there were a number of passages that speak of this:

- John 6:39, *"This is the will of the Father who has sent Me, that of all whom He has given Me, I should lose nothing, but should raise it up at the last day [eschate hemera]."*

- John 6:40, *"This is the will of Him who sent Me, that everyone who sees the Son and believes in Him may have eternal life, and I will raise him up on the last day."*

- John 6:44, *"No one can come to Me unless the Father who has sent Me draw him. And I will raise him up on the last day."*

- John 6:54. *"Whoever eats my flesh and drinks My blood has eternal life. And I will raise him up on the last day."*

- John 11:24, *"Martha said to Him, 'I know that he will rise again in the resurrection on the last day."*

So we see very clearly that the dead in Christ will rise on the Last Day. Therefore, when the Son of Man descends; and the trump of God sounds; and the voice of the Archangel is heard; and the dead in Christ rise; and the believers are caught up, that will unquestionably be on the Last Day—a most specific time.

The Resurrection of Believers and Unbelievers

Furthermore, we noted that John tells us something else is going to happen on the Last Day. In John 12:48, we read, *"He who rejects Me, and does not receive My words, has that which judges him. The word I have spoken will judge him on the last day."* So we see that the judgment of unbelievers is also on the Last Day, which of course, necessitates that the resurrection of unbelievers is also on the Last Day. This also means, of course, that the resurrection of believers and unbelievers are *both* on the Last Day. This is exactly what Jesus tells us in John 5, where He says that the hour is coming when the dead and those that are in the grave will hear His voice and come forth; some to the resurrection of judgment and some to the resurrection of life. There is going to come a general judgment of the saved and the lost that will take place on the Last Day.

So we have seen that on the Last Day the believers will be raised, the unbelievers will be raised, and the judgment will take place, and the Son of Man will come for His own. All of those events are said to take place on the Last Day.

A Third Line of Evidence

We also have a third line of evidence to consider—the Tribulation. When we look at Matthew 24:21 we read of a *"great tribulation, such as has not happened since the beginning of the world until now, no nor shall ever be."* Now, the question is: when is that tribulation in relationship to the coming of the Son of Man. We found in Matthew 24:30 that the same events that are described in 1 Thessalonians 4:16 (namely the Rapture) occur. The Son of Man comes, the sound of the trumpet and the voice of the Archangel are heard, and the gathering together of God's elect take place. Here in Matthew 24 is another picture of the same four events, which are called the Rapture. When will these take place? Verse 29 right before that tells us *"Immediately after the tribulation of those days, 'the sun will be darkened, the moon will not give its light; the stars will fall from heaven, and the powers of the heavens will be shaken. Then the sign of the Son of Man will appear in heaven, . . . and they will see the Son of Man coming . . ."* So we saw that the Son of Man would come **after** the Tribulation.

Now at this point, I think it's very important to remember that the Bible does not confuse "tribulation" and "wrath." These are two entirely different Greek words: *thlipsis* and *orgé* and these mean entirely different things. The Bible says that Jesus said, *"In the world you will have tribulation. But be of good cheer. I have overcome the world"* (John 16:33). The Bible says on the other hand, that God has not appointed us unto wrath but to the obtaining of salvation. The Israelites were in Egypt when the tribulation was on Egypt, but they were out of Egypt when the wrath of God destroyed the entire Egyptian army. And we shall be out of this world when the wrath of God comes upon it. The wrath of God is God's punishment upon unbelievers.

Jesus Christ took the wrath of God for us, and we shall never have to endure the wrath of God.

There is another thing about this passage in Matthew 24 that is worth noting. In Matthew 24:21 it says there shall be great tribulation, and *"Unless those days were shortened, no one would be saved. But for the sake of the elect those days will be shortened."* It's interesting to note that one of the reasons for the shortening of the Tribulation is for the sake of the elect, so it's obvious that the elect or believers are there in the midst of that.

Another Time Signal

Another chronological or time signal in this particular passage as to when this is going to take place is found in verse 29, where it says that the sun will be darkened and the moon will not give her light and the stars will fall from Heaven, and *then* the sign of the Son of Man will appear. As we saw previously in Revelation 6:12-17, you have the picture of the opening of the 6th seal, and we find the same description: the sun will be black as sackcloth, and the moon will become as blood, and the stars of heaven will fall from heaven, and the heavens shall be rolled up as a scroll. And then they will say to the mountains and the hills, *"Fall on us, and hide us from the face of Him who sits on the throne, and from the wrath of the Lamb, for the great day of His wrath has come. Who is able to withstand it?"*

So we see that this eschatological picture of the darkening of the sun and the moon and the falling of the stars of heaven is a prelude to the final judgment of God. And again we see that the Son of Man coming to gather his elect is taking place in the midst of the darkening of the sun and the moon and the falling of the stars which is the consummation of the age, and it is therefore, at the end. The final judgment was at the Last Day. So we see a perfect harmony in all of these passages.

The Thief in the Night

Now this brings us to "the thief in the night." In Matthew 24, which we have been considering, we also read about a thief. The Bible frequently speaks of Christ coming as a thief or as a thief in the night. It says that if the owner of the house had known what hour the thief would come, he would have watched and would not have let his house to be broken into. *"Therefore, you also must be ready, for in an hour when you least expect, the Son of Man is coming."* So what does this have to do with the whole question that we're considering?

In Revelation 1:7 we read, *"Look! He is coming with clouds, and every eye will see Him, even those who pierced Him. And all the tribes of the earth will mourn because of Him. Even so, Amen."* Do you see the contrast in these passages? In one, His coming is as a thief in the night, and in the other, He comes so every eye sees Him, and they that pierced Him and all the tribes of the earth mourn. There seems to be enough distinction in these two passages that those who hold to other views on this say that the passage we just read in Revelation describes the revelation of Christ, when He is revealed, and these other passages that speak of the thief in the night deal with the secret, silent Rapture of Christ when He simply comes into the air and takes the unbelievers out. Therefore, from this they build up their doctrine of the secret, silent coming of Christ, who comes stealthily as a thief in the night. You can picture a thief in the night, clothed in black with rubber shoes creeping silently unseen, unheard to do his work. So this is used as a description of the Rapture and supposedly as an evidence of the fact that there are two different comings, because you have two very different kinds of descriptions. Right?

The Day of the Lord Will Come Like a Thief

Well, maybe, if you happen to be one that is easily fooled, and if you don't bother to do what the Bereans did, who were of a noble mind to search the Scriptures to see if these things be so. But that's the picture that is painted, but is it biblical? I say, "No way." What does the Scripture say? Let's take a look at 2 Peter 3:10: "*But the day of the Lord will come like a thief in the night.*" Stealthily, silently, to catch away His own and no one will know it will happen. As someone described it—in the front page of newspapers the next day when people wake up and their daughter or wife are gone from the house and people finding all sorts of individuals are missing and they don't know what happened, there will be big headlines: "Where did all these millions of people disappear to?" Nobody knew anything was happening! It was a thief in the night. Yes—the Lord *will* come as a thief in the night—in which the heavens will pass away with a great noise and the elements will melt with fervent heat, and the earth also and the works therein will be burned up.[1] But I want to tell you there are not going to be any newspapers published the next day!

In 1 Thessalonians 5 we have one of the classic passages on this subject: "*Concerning the times and the seasons, brothers, you have no need that I write to you. For you know perfectly that the day of the Lord will come like a thief in the night. When they say, 'Peace and safety!' then sudden destruction will come upon them as labor upon a woman with child, and they shall not escape. But you, brothers are not in darkness so that this Day should overtake you as a thief. You are all the sons of light and the sons of the day. We are not of the night nor of the darkness. Therefore let us not sleep as others do. But let us be alert and sober. For those who sleep, sleep at night, and those who get drunk, are drunk at night. But let us, who are of the day, be sober, putting on the breastplate of faith and love, and as a helmet, the hope of salvation. For God has not appointed us to wrath, but to obtain salvation by our Lord Jesus Christ . . ."* (1 Thessalonians 5:1-9).

Some Will Be Watching

Note, my friends, of whom is this passage speaking? There are the believers who are watching for this, and for them Christ does not come as a thief in the night because they are watching, and they know that He is to come and they are watchful and waiting for His coming. But notice also that unbelievers are involved, for they will say "Peace and safety," and then sudden destruction will come upon them when Christ comes as a thief in the night. Now, what about those people who are printing that front page of the paper for the next day? They will never get a picture because the next day will never come. God will stop the wheel of time and start the wheel of eternity. No, the unbelievers are not going to be around here for some long period. When they shall say "Peace," sudden destruction will come upon them.

Revelation 16:15 is another passage that speaks of Jesus coming as a thief. This is an example of an image that you frequently see in the Scripture. *"Look, I am coming as a thief. Blessed is he who watches and keeps his garments on, lest he walk naked and his shame be exposed.*" In the verses following, we read that the seventh angel poured out his vial into the air and a loud voice came out of the temple of heaven from the throne, saying, "It is done."

So these passages that we have looked at in 2 Peter, in 1 Thessalonians, and in Matthew all show that when Christ comes back as a thief in the night, he comes back to bless those that are watching and waiting for Him, and He comes back to destroy the unbeliever and to bring upon them sudden destruction. When He comes as a thief in the night, the stars will fall from the heavens, then the heavens will be burned up, and the end of the world will come.

He Will Take His Own First

Again we see that concomitant with the Second Coming of Jesus Christ, there is the end of the world and the destruction of the wicked and the final judgment. It is also interesting to note that believers will still be there, but since we are not appointed unto wrath, we will be taken to be with the Lord before that wrath is poured out.

In all four of the lines of evidence that we have looked at thus far, we have seen that the same thing is taught. I trust that it will become even more conclusive as we look at the remaining ones, that in the final day, in that great Last Day when Jesus Christ comes, He will take His own out and others will be left. They will be left as Christians are taken up into the air, as the graves are opened and the believing dead are caught up, as Christ comes back with the souls of the saints, and they are joined together in one with the Lord, and as the Lord approaches this earth, and we read that He is going to destroy the world with everlasting fire.

Flaming Fire of Vengeance

There is one other passage that I would still like to consider before closing this section. It is found in 2 Thessalonians 1:7-10 where we read, ". . . *and to give you who are troubled rest with us when the Lord Jesus is revealed from heaven with His mighty angels, in flaming fire taking vengeance on those who do not know God and do not obey the gospel of our Lord Jesus Christ. They shall be punished with eternal destruction, isolated from the presence of the Lord and from the glory of His power, when He comes, in that Day, to be glorified in His saints and to be marveled at by all those who believe.*"

Notice that it says that when Jesus Christ comes back again, when He is revealed from Heaven, He will take vengeance in flaming fire on two classes of people: those that know not God, and those that obey not the Gospel of the Lord Jesus Christ. You see that ignorance is no excuse. There are those that say, "If people never heard about Christ and they don't know anything about it, they'll be all right." However, here is what will happen to those that know not God, who live in the sinful lusts of their own hearts: those who know not God or obey not the Gospel of Christ will be punished with everlasting destruction from the presence of the Lord and the glory of His power when He shall come to be glorified in His saints and admired in those that believe.

Furthermore, there are those who say that when Jesus Christ shall come—whichever one of the comings they would like to make this to be—that then Christ is going to come and He is going to establish a kingdom where He's going to rule over a mixture of believers and unbelievers. There will be all of these unbelievers who will go for a thousand years, and then they're going to rise up and rebel. My friends, if Christ is taking all of the unbelievers out of the world, and He is destroying all those that know not God, and all of those who obey not the Gospel of Jesus Christ, who is going to be left to establish this kingdom that is going to rise up a thousand years later in rebellion? There will be no one here on this earth, because that will be the great and final Last Day, that cataclysmic conclusion of the ages when Christ will come and the stars will fall from heaven, and the heavens will be burnt up, and the sky shall be rolled up as a scroll, and we shall see the Son of Man coming in great power and glory.

The Day of Grace Will End

Let us stop also to think what that day would be like when Jesus Christ comes—Jesus Christ who made the sun, who made this galaxy, who made the billions of galaxies that inhabit our universe. When He comes, He will come with a glory that will outshine the sun, as the writer said. "What a day it will be when people look up and see the glory of Jesus Christ coming—a brightness in the night, in the day." People say, "How can the whole world see Him?" The whole world sees the sun every day. All Jesus has to do is to come to this world, and as soon as He is seen, the day of grace will have ended.

One thing which is a sad heresy involved in all of these other systems is that they all teach that there is a second chance. My friends, there is no second chance. *Now* is the day of salvation.

Today is the accepted time, and there is coming a time when the door of grace will slam shut and the foolish virgins will be there beating on the door, but that day of grace will have ended. When Jesus Christ comes, and people see Him, and all of the believers and all of the believing dead are caught up out of this world, what panic will fill the hearts of those who are left upon this earth as Jesus Christ comes. But as He draws closer, there will come the moment that He will utter that final word, and with flaming fire, this whole world will be destroyed.

How will it be with you in that day?

---

1 Editor's note: In other messages, Dr. Kennedy notes that this judgment is not the same as complete annihilation. Thus, this burning will not be the final word. This burning of purification will be completed, and then the creation will be reconstituted, glorified, and paradisiacal.

A PRAYER...

Father, if we could but put ourselves into the place of some unbeliever, some relative, some friend, some acquaintance, someone that we know, whose heart will fail him for fear in that day when he will see the sign of the Son of Man coming in heaven, when he shall hear the trumpet of God and the voice of the archangel, and the glory of Christ outshining the sun, and believers are leaving this world and leaving Him left in the field, at the mill, in the office, in the home, on the street, left to face the terrible wrath of the Lamb—when it will be everlastingly too late and the day of grace will have ended forever. Oh, God, knowing the terror that will be theirs, may we be moved with compassion and even now determine to do all we can to bring to them the Gospel of hope and light, while it is yet day. In the Name of Him who loved us and washed us from our sins, and has made us kings and priests unto God and His Father, to Whom be glory and honor now and forevermore. Amen.

CHAPTER FIVE

THE LAST TRUMPET

Listen, I tell you a mystery: We shall not all sleep, but we shall all be changed. In a moment, in the twinkling of an eye, at the last trumpet, for the trumpet will sound, the dead will be raised incorruptible, and we shall be changed. For this corruptible will put on incorruption, and this mortal will put on immortality.

1 CORINTHIANS 15:51-53

I think that there would be general agreement that what is being referred to in 1 Corinthians 15:51-53 is what is sometimes called the Rapture. This is obvious because it is clear that some of us are not going to "sleep," which is biblical phraseology for "*die.*" We will not die, but we will be changed in a moment, in the twinkling of an eye. And that change is a change from the corruptible to the incorruptible—from the mortal to the immortal. We will put on our glorified bodies, which is to take place when Christ comes to receive His own. So there is no doubt of that about which we are speaking, or rather the apostle is speaking here.

Now, the question is this: Is there a time clue as to when this is to take place? I believe that all of the various major passages—and we are trying to look at all the major passages concerning the coming of Christ in what is called the Rapture— that there is an interlocking, like a steel mesh, that locks all of these passages together very, very firmly. So let us look at the link in that chain. I believe the time clue is to be found in the phrase "At the last trumpet." When is this that we will be changed? When is it that we will put on incorruption? When is it that we will not die? When is it that the Rapture will take place? Well, I think that Paul is very clear—it will take place "at the last trumpet." That is, at the sounding of the last trumpet.

Scripture Interprets Scripture

Since we believe that Scripture interprets Scripture, let us look at how that helps us. In the book of Revelation 8:2, we read of a familiar event. "*And I saw the seven angels who stand before God, and seven trumpets were given to them.*" So there are seven trumpets that will sound, and as we read through the next verses we see that the first angel sounded, and the second and third angel sounded, and so forth, and various things happened. Let's move to the last trumpet and find out what happens.

Now remember that it is at the last trumpet that the Rapture will take place. So let's see what the concomitant events are that take place at the sounding of the last trumpet. This is found in Revelation 11:15-18:

The seventh angel sounded, and there were loud voices in heaven, saying, 'The kingdoms of the world have become the kingdoms of our Lord, and of His Christ, and He shall reign forever and ever.' And the twenty-four elders, who sat before God on their thrones, fell on their faces and worshipped God, saying, 'We give You thanks, O Lord God Almighty, who is and was and who is to come, because You have taken Your great power and begun to reign. [Note that the words "who is to come" are not in the Greek text because at this event Christ has come and has taken to Him His great power and has begun to reign.] *And the nations were angry, and Your wrath has come, and the time has come for the dead to be judged and to reward Your servants the prophets and the saints and those who fear Your name, small and great, and to destroy those who destroy the earth."*

What is clearly being described here, I think, is that the day of God's judgment has come; i.e., the day of the judgment of His wrath and reward. You will note here again, a picture of a general judgment—a judgment at which time reward is given to the saints, and wrath is poured out upon the destroyers of the earth.

Only One Judgment

Let me point out to you that throughout the whole of Scripture, there is but one judgment. I used to believe 20 years ago, that there were a number of judgments as some people had taught me and I read in many books. It was not until I took the time to examine every verse in Scripture dealing with the judgment that I concluded that there are dozens and dozens of passages that teach that both the saved and the lost are present at one judgment, and there is no verse anywhere in the Bible that ever teaches that one group of people will be judged at one time and another group will be judged at another time.

Over and over again we see the same thing: the day of judgment and the wrath of God. So we see that the sounding of the seventh trumpet is simultaneous with the day of judgment and brings to pass the day of God's wrath, which is to come upon the world and also the giving of rewards to His servants. We see from this passage that at the sounding of the seventh trumpet—the last trumpet—the time for the dead to be judged has come, the time for the rewarding of the saints, and the time for the destroying of the destroyers. This is the time for God to pour out His wrath upon the wicked and to give His rewards, which are given graciously to the saints; that is to say, the sounding of the seventh trumpet is the sounding forth of the day of judgment—the general judgment. Therefore, we see that the Rapture and the general judgment day are simultaneous.

Four Events Will Take Place

We have noted that the classical passage that is used to

describe the Rapture is 1 Thessalonians 4:16-17. Here we read, *"For the Lord Himself will descend from heaven with a shout, with the voice of the archangel, and with the trumpet call of God. And the dead in Christ will rise first. Then we who are alive and remain shall be caught up together with them in the clouds to meet the Lord in the air. . ."* You will also recall that in Matthew 24 we found that the same four events take place: 1) they would see the Son of Man coming; 2) He would send His angels; 3) there would be the sound of the trumpet; and 4) there would be the gathering together of His elect. Remember also that Matthew 24:29 describes when that takes place, *"Immediately after the tribulation of those days, 'the sun will be darkened, the moon will not give its light; the stars will fall from heaven, and the powers of the heavens will be shaken.' Then the sign of the Son of Man will appear in heaven."* All of these events occur immediately after the tribulation of those days.

It is quite obvious from this passage, since the very same four events are described as are found in 1 Thessalonians 4— the coming of the Son of Man, the angels, the sound of the trumpet, and the gathering together of God's elect—that this is obviously the Rapture. However, for those who believe that the Rapture must take place before the Tribulation, this cannot be the Rapture, since their system must dictate what it is and they cannot let the Scriptures speak for themselves, so they must somehow make this something else other than the Rapture. Therefore, they will say this is not the Rapture; it is the *Second* Second Coming of Christ, or the Revelation, which is going to take place after the Tribulation—in spite of the fact that the very identical event that is described in 1 Thessalonians 4 as the Rapture is spoken of here.

The Same Trumpet

Even if that were not sufficient to make it impossible to be anything other than the Rapture, you have another problem that the trumpet brings to light. We read in Matthew 24:31, *"He will send His angels with a great sound of a trumpet . . ."* So here again we find an angel who is going to make a great sound with the trumpet. Now, my friends, going back to 1 Thessalonians 4, we read in verse 16, *". . . with the voice of the archangel, and with the trumpet call of God. And the dead in Christ will rise first."* Note that both 1 Thessalonians 4:16 and 1 Corinthians 15:51-52 where we read, *". . . but we shall all be changed. In a moment, in the twinkling of an eye, at the last trumpet . . ."* are talking about the Rapture. 1 Thessalonians 4:16 is talking about the Rapture, so we are talking about the same trumpet here, and that trumpet is "the last trumpet," and if the last trumpet takes place at the Rapture, then what trumpet is this supposedly taking place in Matthew 24 at the so-called Revelation, for those who want to have two Second Comings?

So again, we see the impossibility of dividing these into two Second Comings, because if this is "the last trumpet," there can be no further trumpet that is sounded because the last trumpet has already sounded.

The Events of "the Last Day"

As we have looked over these passages, we see that Christ is going to come. He is going to come on the Last Day, as John told us. It will be at the Last Day, and that day is the day of the resurrection of the dead. That day is the day of the resurrection of the righteous and of the unrighteous, John tells us. It is the day of judgment. It is the judgment both of the saved and of the lost. It is the day when Christ shall come to take His own unto Himself. It is at the day of the last trumpet. It is the day when the stars will fall from heaven and the sun will not give her light, and the moon will be turned to blood, and the Heavens will be rolled up as a scroll. It is the final cataclysmic Last Day. It is the judgment day. It is the resurrection day. It is the end of all things as we know them here. It is the final consummation of the ages. It is the day that ushers in eternity. Over and over again, we see from every angle from which we can approach this topic, the inescapable conclusion of the Scriptures as it deals with every single facet concerning this, is that Jesus Christ is going to come back for His own on the Last Day.

We saw previously that what this means for unbelievers is that there is nothing but the certain looking for of judgment when God will destroy them with everlasting fire. In the day when He shall come to be admired in them that believe, all of those who obey *not* the Gospel, and who believe *not* in the Lord Jesus Christ, who know *not* God shall be destroyed with everlasting destruction from the presence of the Lord. That will be the end of all things in this world and there is no second chance. In the moment that His glorious appearing is first seen in the sky, in that moment the day of grace will end. As a great bank vault door slams irrevocably closed, the day of God's grace will be over, and there will be nothing but the certain looking for of judgment. Some will be taken. Two grinding at the mill—one taken. Two working in the field—one taken and the other left. Left for what? Left to see the children of God being taken to meet the Lord in the air, and left to meet the wrath of the Lamb. Left to cry for the mountains to cover them and the hills to hide them from the wrath of the Lamb—of Him who sits upon the throne—when

He shall destroy with everlasting fire all of the unbelievers that are left upon this world.

No "Second Coming" Font

I cannot vouch for the authenticity of this story—it may just be somewhat like a preacher story—I don't know how well it is documented; but the story is that *The New York Times* has a certain typeface that is so large they call it the "Second Coming font," and it is kept in a vault at the newspaper. The claim is that it is to be used for nothing other than the Second Coming of Christ. Well, I find that a little difficult to believe that anybody at *The New York Times* even believes that Jesus Christ is coming back at all. (That goes for *The Washington Post*, too and *The Christian Science Monitor*, and quite a few others that I might mention.) But that they could believe that enough to have had such a print created makes a nice story.

Whether it be true or not, I couldn't tell you. But one thing that I can tell you, if they do have such a typeface, which they intend to use to write something like "Christ Has Come Again," I assure you, they will never use it, because by the time they know that the event has occurred they will be scrambling for the dens in the mountains and for the holes to hide them. They will not in the least be concerned about publishing any headlines at all. For, my friend, the whole thing will be over, and in that day, how will it be with you? Can you say, "Even so, come Lord Jesus, come quickly"? Can you say that?

A young lady said to me at the door this morning, just bubbling with enthusiasm, "You know, tonight you will be baptizing a man that I recently led to Christ." She said, "For the first time in my life I can say, 'Even so, come Lord Jesus. Come quickly,' because for the first time in my life, I know that I won't have to meet Him empty handed!"

A Prayer...

Father, grant unto us that joy and anticipation for that moment when we will hear a trumpet sound as we have never heard a trumpet sound before, and we shall—in that moment and in the twinkling of an eye—be changed. These corrupted and corruptible bodies shall disappear forever, and we shall put on our incorruptible bodies. We shall be changed forevermore into bodies that shall no more know pain, nor sickness, nor sorrow, nor death, and we shall go, oh Christ, to be with You forever in the New Heavens and the New Earth, which You are going to create. We praise You and thank You for that. And we pray, oh God, for those who must face the coming of the brightness of Your glory, and know You not and must look with horror and trembling at the sight of the wrath of the Lamb. Help us to be diligent to win them while there still shines upon us the day of Your grace. In the Name of Him who loved us and who gave Himself for us, Amen.

CHAPTER SIX

THE MILLENNIUM

I saw thrones, and they sat on them, and the authority to judge was given to them. And I saw the souls of those who had been beheaded for their witness of Jesus and for the word of God. They had not worshipped the beast or his image, and had not received his mark on their foreheads or on their hands. They came to life and reigned with Christ for a thousand years. The rest of the dead did not come to life until the thousand years were ended. This is the first resurrection.

REVELATION 20:4-5

Ne now conclude this series of messages on the general theme of the Second Coming of Christ and more particularly the time of the Rapture and the agenda of God as it relates to the other events of the End Times.

In Luke 17 we see that Christ selects two events from the Old Testament as types that describe or foretell or picture His final coming to receive His own. The first one is the days of Noah. It says that it shall be *"just as it was in the days of Noah,"* and we've already discussed that. The second illustration is *"as it was in the days of Lot."* We are told that the coming of the Son of Man would be like it was in the days of Lot. What were those days like? Sodom was a city that was overripe for judgment. Its iniquity had risen up as a stench unto God, and God had come down to judge it. This is the city that has given its name to the sin of homosexuality—sodomy. But before pouring out His judgment, God first determined to rescue from that city Lot and his family, who were believers. So He sent His angels to rescue Lot from this wicked city before it was completely overthrown and destroyed by fire and brimstone. This is a picture in miniature of the coming of Christ to a world that has ripened for judgment and which has become increasingly sinful.

I think it is interesting that in our day we have a resurgence of the sin of Sodomy. And this might make us take heed that today it is surely as it was in the days of Lot. Within a sinful world, the Church is a small remnant, which God will send His angels to deliver before the destruction comes. So this is the picture, the type, which Jesus describes for us.

A Picture of the Church

Now, let us see what time signal we can find here to tell us something about the time of the Rapture. In Luke 17:28, Jesus says, *"they ate, they drank, they bought, they sold, they planted, they built,"* and then see verse 29, *"But on the day that Lot departed from Sodom, fire and brimstone rained from heaven and destroyed them all."* So there is our time secret to let us know something about the agenda of God. We see the same thing that we have seen everywhere else. The same day that Lot went out of Sodom it rained fire and brimstone from Heaven and destroyed them all. So, therefore, if Lot and his family are a picture of the remnant of the Church, which the angel had come to deliver out of the wicked city of destruction, then we can see that in the day that that family of God is taken out by the angel, in that day destruction will come upon them all.

We saw exactly the same thing held true in the days of Noah. In Luke 17:27 we read concerning the days of Noah, *"They were eating, drinking, marrying, and were given in marriage until the day when Noah entered the ark. Then the flood came and destroyed them all."* And in Genesis 7 it says, *"On the very same day"* that Noah entered into the ark, the floodgates of the heavens were opened and all the fountains of the great deep burst open and they were all destroyed.

So, again with Lot, we see the same picture. In fact, this story reminds us that so quickly did that destruction follow upon the heels of their rescue, that Lot's wife who was disobedient and unbelieving turned back and was destroyed in that destruction. So we see that there is no great gap of time after the rescue of God's people before the destruction of the wicked comes.

Those Left Behind

Jesus reminds us of something else in Luke 17:34-36. He says, *"I tell you, on that night two men will be in one bed; the one will be taken and the other will be left. Two women will be grinding grain together; the one will be taken and the other will be left. Two men will be in the field; the one will be taken and the other will be left."* Note that right before this He has said, *"Remember Lot's wife."* This has been used by some to indicate that some people are going to be taken away and then others are going to be left for a period of years in which all sorts of imagined activities are supposed to take place. But the truth of the matter is that this picture is taken right out of the destruction of Sodom and we see that indeed, one was taken, others were left, but they were left for sudden destruction, which came upon them. Noah was taken; the rest were left to face the terror of sudden destruction. Christ will come as a thief in the night to take His own and sudden destruction will come upon the rest.

Were there headlines in the next morning's edition of the *Sodom Daily News* that said: "Lot and Family Mysteriously Disappear. Strange Visitors Are Implicated"? Obviously, those headlines were not in the paper, and quite obviously no such paper as that was ever printed for the same day fire and brimstone fell from Heaven and destroyed them all. So there would have been no editors around to publish any papers if printing had been around for the publishing of papers, which of course it was not.

Left Behind for What?

So we see that when taken in its context, this thought of one being taken and the other left does not by any means leave the impression—which some people would have you think that it leaves—that some people are going to be left around for some long season. Therefore, we can conclude about this passage that what it teaches is that the rescue of Lot and His family by the angel, which Jesus says is a picture of what is sometimes called the Rapture, is to take place on the Judgment Day when judgment is poured out upon the city of destruction. We can see that it is to take place simultaneously on that same day with the end of the world. They were all destroyed. In the case of Noah, the flood took them all away.

It is worth noting also that here we have this picture of one taken and the other left, and yet this is called the day when the Son of Man shall be revealed. So we see that the Rapture and the Revelation of the Son of Man are the same event and that there are not two Second Comings of Jesus Christ, but only one. So this is the sixth passage that we have dealt with concerning the matter of the time of the Rapture.

The Millennium

What, then, does this say concerning the matter of the Millennium? How does that relate to what we are talking about here? The first thing that should be said about the Millennium is that the Bible never mentions such a thing. The Bible never mentions a "Millennium." Why, to hear some people talk, you'd think it was the main theme of the Bible, wouldn't you? But it's not in there.

If you'd turn to the 20th chapter of the book of Revelation, you will see that the Bible mentions several times in that chapter a thousand years. Now you say, "Well, doesn't the Millennium mean a thousand years? Yes, the word "millennium" in Latin, *mille annum*, means "a thousand years." But there is a very important difference and that difference deals not with the *denotation* of the word millennium, which denotes a thousand years, but the *connotation* of the word millennium.

As far as the connotation is concerned, a great matter of interpretation and connotation have been poured into the word millennium until it has a meaning all of its own, which has been given to it by various writers on the subject. Therefore, it is important for us to know that the Bible simply mentions the term of a thousand years, and the Bible doesn't say anything at all about many of the things that people will say refer to the millennium.

The Old Testament Kingdom

Many things are exported from the Old Testament and poured into this concept of a 'millennium.' In the Kingdom of the Old Testament many things are taken from that and poured into the thousand years in Revelation 20 to produce the concept of the Millennium.

So, first of all we should note that in the Old Testament, we never have a thousand year kingdom. The kingdom that the Old Testament talks about is always a Kingdom that lasts forever and ever. It is a Kingdom that has no end. Over and over again this is what we're told in the Old Testament. Here we have an everlasting Kingdom, which cannot very well be forced into the thousand years of Revelation 20, especially if those thousand years are to be interpreted literally as simply a thousand years.

Two Resurrections?

In Revelation 20:4-8 we read, *"I saw thrones, and they sat on them, and the authority to judge was given to them. And I saw the souls of those who had been beheaded for their witness of Jesus and for the word of God. They had not worshipped the beast or his image, and had not received his mark on their foreheads or on their hands. They came to life and reigned with Christ for a thousand years. The rest of the dead did not come to life until the thousand years were ended. This is the first resurrection. Blessed and holy is he who takes part in the first resurrection. Over these the second death has no power, but they shall be priests of God and of Christ and shall reign with Him a thousand years. When the thousand years are ended, Satan will be set free from his prison and will go out to deceive the nations . . ."*

As we go on farther, we see a great white throne, and in verse 12, *". . . the dead, small and great, standing before God."* And verse 13, *"The sea gave up the dead who were in it, and Death and Hades delivered up the dead who were in them. And they were judged, each one by his works."*

So we see a reference to a first resurrection in verse 5, and then in verse 13 there is a reference to another resurrection where the sea gives up the dead that are in it. This leads some to conclude that we will go on from the time of the Rapture until Jesus comes again and then there will be the first resurrection when believers are resurrected. Then there will be a thousand year Millennium, and then the unbelievers will be resurrected. Well, what is the problem with that? There are numerous problems.

One Resurrection and One Judgment

First of all, we have seen over and over again in the Bible that there is one resurrection and one judgment and that both the saved and the lost are present at one judgment, and if they are judged together they are raised together. We have seen that, for example, on the Last Day the believers in Christ will be raised, and on the Last Day the unbelievers will be judged on the same Last Day. Over and over again we see passages where both the saved and lost are judged on the Last Day. The one who had the ten talents is present in the same judgment with the one who received the one talent. To the one with ten talents he says *"Enter the joy of your master."* But he takes the talent of the one who had one talent and gives it to the one who has ten, and he throws him into outer darkness where there will be weeping and gnashing of teeth. Romans 2 talks about the saved and the lost and the saved again. Revelation 11 talks about the final judgment when God will give rewards unto His saints and will destroy the wicked.

So everywhere we see the final judgment is a judgment where the saved and the lost are present. As I told you before, I have on many occasions challenged anyone to produce a single verse in the Bible which says that any people are judged at different judgments at different times, whereas I can produce dozens of passages that clearly state that both the saved and the lost are both judged at the same judgment and are present with each other and with Christ at the very same judgment. So here you have a problem. If the saved and the lost are resurrected and judged at the same time, obviously you have no room for a thousand year millennium.

The Hour Is Now Here

John is the author of the book of Revelation, and Scripture is supposed to interpret Scripture, so let's see what John has to say about this in his gospel. In John 5:24 we read, "*Truly, truly I say to you, whoever hears My word and believes in Him who sent Me has eternal life and shall not come into condemnation, but has passed from death into life.*" To pass from death unto life is a resurrection. Indeed, in this case it is a spiritual resurrection. Those who hear the Word of God and believe are spiritually regenerated or spiritually resurrected. He that believes passes from death unto life. Believers are those who are said to present themselves unto God as those who are alive from the dead. "*You hath He quickened [made alive], who were dead in trespasses and sins*" (Ephesians 2:1 KJV).

Continuing in verse 25 of John 5, "*Truly, truly I say to you, **the hour is coming, and is now here** when the **dead** will hear the voice of the Son of God, and those who hear will live. For as the Father has life in Himself, so He has given to the Son to have life in Himself, and has given Him authority to execute judgment also, because He is the Son of Man.*" So we see that Jesus has life in Himself, and He speaks His word, and those who hear it and believe it are quickened from the deadness of their sins and passed from death unto life. This is a spiritual resurrection.

The Hour Is Coming in the Future

But Jesus continues, and we read in verse 28, "*Do not marvel at this.*" If you think this is incredible that the spiritually dead are now made alive as they hear the voice of the Son of God, marvel not at this, "*for the hour is coming . . .*" Now you'll notice that something is omitted this time. In verse 25 we read *"the hour is coming, and is now here . . . "* In verse 28, you notice that the words *"and is now here"* are omitted. The hour is coming— this is not the present; this is future. Sometime in the future ***"the hour is coming** in which **all who are in the graves** will hear His voice and will come out—those who have done good to the resurrection of life, and those who have done evil to the resurrection of judgment"* (John 5:28-29).

We see that an hour is coming. Take note that it says, *"all who are in the graves."* You see, first it was the spiritually dead who are spiritually made alive. Now it is those who are in the graves. These are the bodies of believers who are raised. One was a spiritual resurrection and it was a spiritual quickening of the spiritually dead. Then there is a future resurrection, and it is those who are in the graves. They shall come forth, and you'll notice that it is ***"the hour** . . . in which all who are in the graves will . . . come out,"* some to the resurrection of life and some to the resurrection of judgment. The smallest period of time—an hour—is given as the time in which this will take place.

A Spiritual Resurrection

So we see that according to John 5, we have a spiritual resurrection, which began when Jesus began to preach His Word and has continued for several thousand years since then. When the Word of Christ is proclaimed and people hear that word and believe, they pass from death unto life. They are spiritually resurrected and present themselves unto God as those who are alive from the dead. This is a spiritual resurrection. That is the first resurrection.

Now it is altogether fitting and proper that this should be so, because what was the first death that man experienced? The first death that mankind experienced was a spiritual death. *"In the day that you eat from it you will surely die,"* and Adam ate, and he died . . . 900 years later. Or did he? The truth is, he died that very hour—spiritually he died. So the first death that man experienced was a spiritual death. So too the first resurrection that man experiences is a spiritual resurrection. Each one of you who is a true believer has already experienced a spiritual resurrection from the dead. *"You, being dead in your sins . . . He has resurrected together with Him, having forgiven you all sins,"* Colossians 2:13 tells us.

The First Resurrection Is Spiritual

Some will say, "Well, would not this be a spiritualizing of the passage, because though John 5 talks about a spiritual resurrection that began to take place when Christ preached His Word, does not Revelation 20 talk about the resurrection of the bodies of people?" Revelation 20:4 says, *"I saw thrones, and they sat on them, and the authority to judge was given to them. And I saw **the souls** of those who had been beheaded for their witness of Jesus and for the word of God. They had not worshipped the beast or his image, and had not received his mark on their foreheads or on their hands. They came to life and reigned with Christ for a thousand years. The rest of the dead did not come to life until the thousand years were ended. **This is the first resurrection.**"* Now, if you were to diagram that sentence, what John is saying is, "I saw the souls of them, they lived and reigned with Christ a thousand years. This is the first resurrection."

What is John talking about here in Revelation? Is he talking about bodies? Or is he talking about souls? Obviously, he's talking about souls. He's talking about the very same thing that he was talking about first of all in John 5—a spiritual resurrection. We who have received Christ have taken part in this spiritual resurrection, and we live and reign with Christ. We are kings and priests unto God and His Father right now. Notice also that it continues in verse 6: *"Blessed and holy is he who takes part in the first resurrection. Over these the second death has now power, but they shall be priests of God and of Christ and shall reign with Him a thousand years."*

A Second General Resurrection

Then at the end of the passage in Revelation 20 we have another resurrection. *"And I saw the dead, small and great . . . The sea gave up the dead who were in it, and Death and Hades delivered up the dead who were in them. And they were judged, each one by his works. . . . Anyone whose name was not found written in the Book of Life was cast into the lake of fire"* (Revelation 20:12-13, 15). Here you have the same event that is described in the 5th chapter of John. The hour is coming in the future when all of those who are in the graves, all of the bodies of the dead, whether they are in the graves or in the sea or wherever they are, will be resurrected, both the saved and the lost, and they will come forth to judgment.

We have seen over and over again that in every instance the Bible teaches a general judgment at which are present both the saved and the lost. In this instance, those whose names are found written in the Book of Life go on to eternal life, and those whose names are not found written in the Book of Life are cast into the Lake of Fire. So we find in Revelation 20 the same event referred to that we found in John 5. In John 5, of course, there is also reference to a spiritual resurrection of the souls of those who believe, and then there is a general resurrection of the bodies of believers and unbelievers.

In Revelation 20 we see first of all that the first resurrection is a resurrection of the soul. Then later there is a general resurrection of the bodies of believers and unbelievers. I should point out that in verse 5, where it says *"This is the first resurrection,"* in the Greek text *this* is in an emphatic position. So what he is saying is this: "I saw the souls of them. They lived and reigned with Christ a thousand years. **This** is the first resurrection," as if to preclude any conclusions of any other sort that something else is the first resurrection.

"A Thousand Years" and Biblical Numerology

But what then is meant by the phrase "a thousand years"? You need to understand something about biblical numerology—and the nature of the apocalyptic literature that you find in Daniel and Ezekiel and Revelation—which is very symbolic in nature. The Bible uses numbers in a very highly symbolic fashion. Of course, it often uses them very literally, but in apocalyptic literature in particular, it uses numbers as it does other things very symbolically.

We see that three is the number of God. Four is the number of the earth—the four winds, the four corners of the earth, etc. Six is the number of man, and 666 is the epitome of the fallenness of man—one less than perfection. Seven is the number of perfection. Ten is the number of completion. Twelve is the number of the Church. Twelve times twelve, 144 is the totality of the Church, the Old and New Testament. Ten times ten times ten equals a thousand, which is the complete totality of the time which is involved. For example this is clearly seen in the Psalms where we read that God tells His people not to bring Him all of their oblations, sacrifices, and burnt offerings. He says He wearies of them. He says He owns the cattle upon a thousand hills. Now someone once said to me one time, "When the Bible says a thousand, it doesn't mean a thousand and one. It means a thousand." Is that true?

When the book of Revelation talks about the seven spirits of God, I would ask you, does God have seven spirits, or does He have one spirit? Is He talking about the seven-fold perfections of the Holy Spirit, which He most certainly is, and not some seven spirits of God and then the Son and the Father, and now we get into a "none-ity," instead of a Trinity. No—what does the Psalmist mean when He says God owns the cattle upon a thousand hills? Does he mean that God doesn't own the cattle upon a thousand and one hills? Of course not. What does that actually mean? It means God owns the cattle on all hills. For that matter, it means that God owns the cattle in the valleys, too. Not only that, but God owns the hills, the trees on the hills, and the gold under the hills. What that verse actually means is that God owns everything, and He doesn't need anything that we have to give to Him.

The Totality of Time

So, therefore, "a thousand years" is the totality of time; it is a large and indeterminate; i.e., unspecified amount of time between the first coming of Christ and the Second Coming of Christ. It is the entire, what is called the Inter-Advental

Period between the first Advent and the second Advent of Christ. The length of that time is unknown. It is a long period of time obviously, but it is unspecified as to exactly how long it is, and during all of this time—since we experienced this first resurrection—we began to reign with Christ as priests and kings under God. All of this time we reign with Him; partly here on the earth and partly in Heaven when we are translated to go to be with Him when we die. Whether it started back there for some of the early ones, and then more, and then more, and down the centuries, it has continued; first on the earth and then in Heaven with a great body of saints above.

This, I believe—as you compare scripture with scripture—is the picture that is being described right here in Revelation 20, which has been the opinion that has been most generally held by the Church down through the centuries. It was the view that was held by Martin Luther. It was the view that was held by Calvin. It was the view that was held by John Knox, and the view that was held by John Wesley. It was the view that basically is found in all of the great confessions of the Church. It is the view that is found in the Westminster Confession of Faith, which teaches a general judgment and general resurrection.

Summary and Conclusion

So in conclusion, concerning the matter of Rapture—as we move back to that now, after considering the Millennium—we have looked at Sodom and the Rapture, and we have seen that in the very same day that the believers were taken out of the city of destruction that fire and brimstone came and they were destroyed. Even so, the Rapture is concomitant with the judgment and the destruction of the wicked. Also, we have looked at Noah and the Rapture, and we saw again that on the selfsame day that Noah and his family representing the remnant of believers were taken out—then destruction came upon the world and all of the wicked were destroyed.

The Time of the Rapture: We looked at the time of the Rapture and we turned our attention to 1 Thessalonians 4, which is the classic passage for that. We are told that the dead in Christ shall rise first, and then we who are alive and remain shall be caught up together with the Lord. We saw that the time clue there was that the dead in Christ will rise. Then we went to the gospel of John, and we found when that would be. We found that five times over Jesus said that those who believe in Him, He would raise them up at the Last Day. *"He that eats my flesh and drinks my blood, I will raise Him up in the last day."* We read that He would lose none that the Father had given him, but He would raise them up in the Last Day, and five times over He says that on *the Last Day* He would raise up the believers. Also we are told in the same gospel that on the Last Day He would judge the wicked. So we see from this passage that the Rapture is simultaneous—*on the same day*—with the resurrection of the dead and with the judgment of the wicked, and it is the Last Day.

The Tribulation: We looked at the Tribulation and the Rapture and we looked at Matthew 24, which is the only passage in the Bible that deals with both the Tribulation and the Rapture. We saw that it says, *"Immediately after the tribulation of those days, 'the sun will be darkened, the moon will not give its light . . . and they will see the Son of Man coming . . . with a great sound of a trumpet, and they shall gather His elect from the four winds"* (Matthew 24:29-31). Now people try to avoid the force of that by saying, "Well, that doesn't refer to the Rapture," and I have said over and over again: You have the same four elements that you have in 1 Thessalonians 4—the Lord Himself will descend, the angels of God, the trumpet of God, the gathering together of His elect. So if that isn't the Rapture in Matthew 24, what makes you think it's the Rapture in 1 Thessalonians 4?

My friends, does language not have any meaning at all? But if it violates their system, it seems that some people do not want to believe it. Furthermore, we find that the passage in Matthew 24 says, *"with a great sound of a trumpet,"* and if that's supposed to be an event that takes place after the Rapture—because the last trumpet will sound at the Rapture—there can be no further trumpet and that cannot be an event seven years later. It is the Rapture, and that takes place immediately after those days.

The Thief in the Night: We looked at "the thief in the night." We are told that there is a "silent" and "secret" Rapture that is coming when people will be taken away and others will wake up in the morning and wonder where everybody went, and there will be a great hubbub about that. But we find in 2 Peter 3:10 that *"the day of the Lord will come like a thief in the night, in which the heavens will pass away with a loud noise."* So it is not something silent and secret. It comes suddenly upon the unbelievers, but as we're told in Thessalonians, we are not the children of darkness. It is not going to come suddenly upon us. But when it does come as a thief in the night, it will come with destruction. So we see that when the Lord comes as a thief in the night and takes His own away, also in that day the heavens will be destroyed, the moon will not give its light, the sun will be darkened, the stars will fall from heaven, and we have the end of the world.

The Last Trumpet: We found as we examined 1 Corinthians 15:51-53 that the trumpet shall sound—"the last trumpet," which will be the last trumpet, and then *"we shall all be changed. In a moment, in the twinkling of an eye,"* and we will put on incorruption. So we see that the Rapture is to take place at the last trumpet, and in Revelation 11 we saw that the last trumpet took place at the judgment of the earth, when the time of His wrath has come and He will give rewards unto the saints and destroy those that destroy the earth. So the last trumpet is the announcement of the final judgment of God, which again is a general judgment at which are present the saved and the lost. Furthermore, we see that if the last trumpet takes place at the Rapture, then these passages, which they sometimes use to deal with the Revelation subsequent to that, will not work because they have a trumpet too, but the last trumpet has already sounded. So it is the same last trumpet as at the Rapture, and the Revelation of Christ is on the same day.

Conclusion: So in conclusion, we can say that I believe that the Bible teaches that we shall see the sign of the Son of Man coming in heaven, and the Son of Man Himself shall descend and there will be the voice of the Archangel, and there will be the Trumpet of God, and the believers shall be caught up in the air to be with Jesus Christ. The dead in Christ shall arise, and the unbelievers shall be left—some in the office, some in the shop, some in the fields, some in the home, some in the bed. They shall be left, but they shall be left not to continue their lives and print newspapers and carry on their activities for years. But they shall be left to face horror and terror.

A PRAYER...

Heavenly Father, as we conclude this series on the End Times, we pray that we may not only watch and be ready for the return of Your Son, Jesus Christ, but that knowing the imminent destruction facing all those who do not know Christ, we will be zealous to share the Gospel with all whom we have an opportunity to reach, for only through knowing Christ can they be saved from the wrath to come.

May we also seek to be salt and light to our culture, bringing the redeeming light of biblical truth to every area of life, for while we cannot know the day or hour when Christ will return, we know that our task now is to glorify God in every aspect of our lives and to enjoy our relationship with Him, both now and forever, and in so doing may we hear the words, "Well done, good and faithful servant," at His return.